SO-AAE-535

What Does a CITIZEN Do?

What Does a Taxpayer Do?

Enslow Publishing
101 W. 23rd Street
Suite 240
New York, NY 10011
USA

enslow.com

Chris Townsend

Published in 2019 by Enslow Publishing, LLC.
101 W. 23rd Street, Suite 240, New York, NY 10011

Library of Congress Cataloging-in-Publication Data

Names: Townsend, Chris, author.
Title: What does a taxpayer do? / Chris Townsend.
Description: New York : Enslow Publishing, [2019] | Series: What does a citizen do? | Audience: Grade level 5–8. | Includes bibliographical references and index.
Identifiers: LCCN 2017055218| ISBN 9780766098756 (library bound) | ISBN 9780766098763 (pbk.)
Subjects: LCSH: Taxation—United States—Juvenile literature.
Classification: LCC HJ2362 .T69 2018 | DDC 336.200973—dc23
LC record available at https://lccn.loc.gov/2017055218

Printed in the United States of America

CONTENTS

Calculating and filing your taxes may not be much fun, but taxpayer money funds necessary state and federal infrastructure and programs, from the roads we drive on to the military serving the United States.

Introduction

Have you ever thought about who pays for roads? Who buys all those books in the library? What about the courthouse or the city hall? Where does the money for schools come from? The short answer is everyone helped pay for them. Anyone who earns money or buys something pays money to the government to help pay for all those things and more. Without taxes who would pay for all the things from which we all benefit? Taxes are an important tool to pay for things we all share. They also pay for our government and military.

In a civic society, everyone contributes to the common good. One of the ways citizens contribute to their society is through paying taxes. This book looks at what a taxpayer does. It may seem simple at first glance. A taxpayer pays taxes. But why? And how? Who gets all that money? What do they use it for? What if you don't pay? This book will provide answers to those questions and more. Without taxes, there would be no money to pay for a government or many of the things we all enjoy. We are all safer because we pay the taxes used to buy tanks and ships and pay soldiers, sailors, airmen, marines, police, firefighters, and many more people who work for the government.

What Does a Taxpayer Do?

Chapter one looks at the history of taxes in America. Taxes were one of the main reasons America went to war against Britain. Today, taxes are a normal part of everyday life. Chapter two explores who has to pay taxes. Anyone who earns enough money or buys things in a store needs to know how taxes affect them. Chapter three explains the various types of taxes that taxpayers pay. There are city taxes, state taxes, federal taxes, sales taxes, property taxes, and even something called the death tax! Chapter four outlines many of the things for which taxes are used. They probably paid for this book you are reading right now! Taxes also pay for many things from which all citizens benefit but for which no one pays directly. Chapter five is all about how taxes get paid and what can happen if they are not paid. Tax violations brought down some of the worst criminals in America!

One day you will need to understand what taxes are for and how to pay them. If you've ever bought anything from a store you probably already paid taxes. But taxes can be difficult to understand. The laws that explain what to pay and how to pay can fill a very large book. Taxes do not have to be hard. This book will explain taxes simply. After reading this book, you will understand how our system of taxes came about. If you really like taxes and numbers maybe you can be an accountant and help other people with their taxes. There are even tax lawyers who only work on cases about taxes and financial advisers who help people plan for taxes.

History of Taxes

Americans have not always paid taxes. In fact, unfair taxes were one of the reasons for the American Revolution! Taxes have changed a lot over the years. At first, taxes were for goods like tea. Now we have a whole system of taxes on everything from purchases to income. There is a whole office in the government to make sure we pay our taxes. How did we get from there to here? This chapter will explore the history of taxes in America. We all enjoy the benefits from taxes. Our modern system evolved over two hundred years.

Early Taxes

Unfair taxes were one of the main reasons America declared its independence from England. The trouble began in 1765 with the Stamp Act. The Stamp Act placed a tax on all printed papers. The tax even included playing cards! Britain had a lot of debt from its war with France. America protested because the Stamp Act was a direct tax and Americans had no voice in the British government. The Stamp Act was removed in 1766. But the fight flared again in

AND A MEETING WAS HELD, WHERE THE PROCLAMATION WAS READ, THAT HAD CAUSED ALL THIS PERTURBATION.

Early American colonists were angry about Great Britain's taxation of products like tea.

1767 with the Townshend Acts. The Townshend Acts avoided the direct tax issue by instead calling it an import tax. Any goods coming to America, like tea, glass, lead, paper, and paint were taxed. The Americans protested again. All of the taxes except for the tax on tea were removed. The tax on tea remained a sore point. In protest, some Americans threw tea in the harbor. The American Revolution soon followed and ended Britain's right to tax the new nation of America.

After the revolution, America had to figure out how to pay for all of the debt created by the war. The government was facing

Boston Tea Party

The tax on tea led to more smuggling. Smugglers would bring their tea in without paying the taxes and sell it for less. The British passed a law that allowed their company to sell tea for even less. The Americans were not happy. They wanted the royal governor, Thomas Hutchinson, to refuse to allow the British tea into America for sale. John Adams held a meeting. Thousands came to the meeting. When the people at the meeting heard that the governor wouldn't send the tea back to Britain, they got angry. The people poured out of the meeting and toward the harbor. They threw all of the tea into the harbor. It was called the Boston Tea Party.

The new US government wanted to pay off the national debt by taxing whiskey, but many citizens objected, leading to the Whiskey Rebellion.

the same problem that led to Britain ordering a tax. Many States had debt from the war that they were unable to pay. The secretary of treasury, Alexander Hamilton, wanted to combine all of the states' debt into a single national debt. It was a contentious debate. Wealthier states like Virginia did not want to have to pay for other states' share of the debt.[1] In 1790, Congress voted to gather all of the states' debts under a single national debt. Alexander Hamilton wanted to pay this debt by taxing whiskey and other alcohol. Congress agreed, but the tax led to a brief conflict known as the Whiskey Rebellion. Thomas Jefferson removed the tax once he became president. The United States chose to continue to raise revenue through tariffs. Tariffs are fees charged on goods brought into the United States. This system worked until the Civil War when the debt again became too large to handle.

What Does a Taxpayer Do?

National Tax

Over the next few decades there was no national income tax. After the French Revolution, America decided not to pay its debt. The debt was to the old king, and he was no longer around. France was not happy, and war was brewing between the United States and France. Congress created a national property tax to raise money. In 1812, The United States and Britain went to war again. The United States raised money for the war by raising import taxes and fees on sugar, tobacco, coffee, and alcohol. When the Civil War started, these small taxes were not enough. In 1861, Congress passed the first national income tax. Anyone who made more than $800 had to pay taxes.[2] The tax helped to pay for the Civil War. In 1872, the tax was removed. Congress passed another national tax in 1894, but it was removed by the Supreme Court. The Constitution requires any tax to be linked to the number of people in the state.

As World War I loomed, a new tax was needed. In 1913, Congress changed the Constitution to allow for a national income tax with no restrictions. Then, Congress passed a new national income tax for anyone who made more than $3,000. That may not seem like a lot, but money changes over time. Three thousand dollars from 1913 is worth over $70,000 today! Since WWI there has always been an income tax. People who made little money did not have to pay. The more money someone makes the more they pay. Having a tax system means needing someone to run it. Someone has to count all that money and make sure it is the right amount! That someone is the Internal Revenue Service (IRS).

IRS

When Congress created the first income tax during the Civil War, they hired a commissioner of internal revenue. Even though the tax was removed the position stayed. In 1913, when a permanent income tax passed, the Bureau of Internal Revenue was created. The bureau was responsible for making all the rules about how to pay taxes. They created tax forms for people to fill out when paying

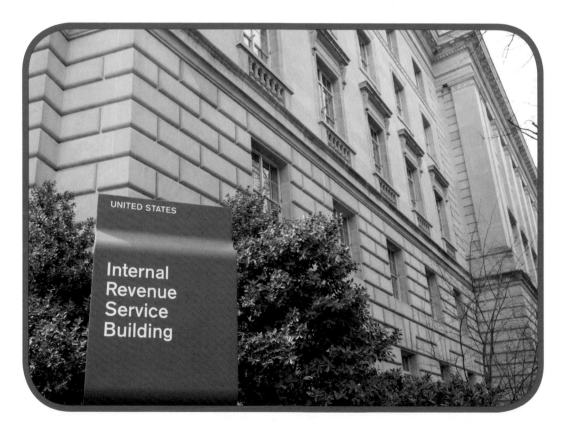

UNITED STATES

Internal Revenue Service Building

The Internal Revenue Service, otherwise known as the IRS, has been around since 1913. It oversees tax collection in the United States.

taxes. The forms let people figure out their own taxes. Previously, people called tax collectors individually determined and collected taxes for the government. The new system let people calculate their taxes and pay them to the government. Every year on April 15, taxes are due to the government.

Since 1913, The IRS has grown into a large part of the government. As America has grown wealthier, the amount of taxes paid has grown. In 2015, the IRS received over $3.3 trillion in taxes from the American people and businesses.[3] That seems like a lot until you realize the US government spent $500 million more than that! The IRS takes the money that it collects and uses it to pay for many things. Anyone who works for the government is paid from this money. This can mean military members or government workers, like senators. Even the president is paid from this money. The IRS also distributes money to pay for education and health insurance. Money is also used to pay for roads and bridges. In the next chapter, we'll talk about who has to pay taxes

Who Pays Taxes?

Nearly everyone pays taxes. Most pay taxes on money they earn. Almost all pay a sales tax when they buy something. Even if there is no sales tax, companies still include the cost of taxes in their prices. Even if you trade things and no money changes hands there may still be taxes! Profits from a business or the sale of an item also require taxes. If it seems like taxes are everywhere, remember what Benjamin Franklin said: "In this world nothing can be said to be certain except death and taxes."[1]

Income Earners

When the tax laws were first introduced, they called for taxes on lawful income. Soon, the government realized it had ignored the money made by criminals. The tax code was changed to account for all income to fix the gap. It turned out that criminals like Al Capone were making a lot of money. They were making billions of dollars by today's standards. Since their income was not lawful, early tax laws

US citizens who make above a certain amount of money must pay income tax, which is a percentage of the income they have earned from working over the course of a single year.

did not think about this income. When Al Capone got sent to jail it wasn't for his crimes. Al Capone went to jail for not paying his taxes!

Any person who makes money has to pay taxes on that money. This usually takes the form of taxes on his or her salary. When you work, your company takes a portion of your money and sends it to the government. At the end of the year you file a form. If you were supposed to pay less you get money back. If you didn't pay enough you owe money. If the IRS decides that someone has not paid enough they can take the money out of their paycheck. They can even take away a person's house!

Income earners also pay taxes when they buy stuff or if they own things of value, like a house. Most states have a sales tax that charges you a little extra when you buy anything. This is why if you try to buy something that costs one dollar you'd better have more than one dollar on you! Property is also taxed every year. Each year, a tax person will come and decide how much a house or property is worth. A portion of that value must be paid as taxes. Anyone who sells a house or anything else for profit has to pay taxes on the money they made from the sale.

Businesses

People are not the only ones who pay taxes. Businesses that earn money in the United States all have to pay taxes on the money they earn. Some businesses are just people who make or sell things. Other businesses make billions and have thousands of employees. If people give you money for something you sold or something you did for them, you have a business. Any business that makes a profit has to pay taxes on the money that they earn. Business taxes can be very difficult. Most businesses use an accountant. An accountant is a person who specializes in money.

Businesses have expenses. This is all the money the business spends to operate. It can include salaries, rent, and any money spent on the business. These expenses are usually taken out of how much a business owns. If a business makes a $1,000 in a month but spends $300 on salaries and another $300 on other costs, then they would owe taxes only on the $400. This keeps businesses from having to pay taxes based only on the amount of money they take in. Of course, some businesses are very good at figuring out costs. Some companies end up paying no tax because they can show that they made no actual profit!

Anyone can start a business. A business can just be one person who makes something or provides a service. These are the simplest types of companies. If you mow your neighbor's lawn and get twenty dollars for your trouble, you technically have a business. If you mow twenty lawns in a year and all your neighbors pay you twenty dollars you may have to pay taxes on that money.[2] Now, if you paid for the lawnmower and the gas or had any other costs associated with your business, you can deduct those expenses. If your profit is less than $400 you do not have to pay taxes. You still have to file a tax form with the IRS to prove your expenses. If the IRS doubts your claim, they can audit you. In an audit, a person or business has to prove everything they claimed as a deduction.

Nonprofits

Some companies do not have to pay taxes. These companies are usually charities or churches who make no profit. They are called nonprofits. Just because a company is not making money does not make it a nonprofit company. A nonprofit company spends all the extra money it earns toward its mission or goal. This does not mean everyone

Nonprofit organizations like churches do not have to pay taxes on the donations they receive.

Tax on Trades

Long before money was used for buying things people traded goods. Let's say I raise chickens. I have all the eggs I can eat. Some mornings I would like milk with my eggs. I don't have a cow. If my friend has a cow, I can give her eggs for some milk. This type of trade is called bartering. Even though there is no profit involved, it does not count as a nonprofit. Since the IRS considers any form of income as taxable, I may have to pay taxes on the value of the milk I received!

who works there works for free. The staff gets paid first, along with any other costs. Any money left over has to be spent on the goal of the company.

Churches (this includes temples, mosques, and synagogues) are a common example of a nonprofit. Many people like to donate money to their church. In 2015, Americans gave almost $120 million to churches and other worship locations.[3] Sometimes this is money collected at each service. Some churches have a regular system for members to donate a portion of their paychecks. As long as the church uses all this money on its religious mission, it pays no taxes. People who receive a paycheck from the church still have to pay taxes on their income. In the next chapter, we'll explore all the different types of taxes.

Types of Taxes

The United States collects taxes in many different forms. There are taxes paid when you buy things. This is called a sales tax. There are also local taxes that the city and state charges on income and property. Finally, there are national taxes that are paid on income or any other type of gains. These taxes are used for a wide variety of functions, from paying salaries for government workers to public goods like libraries and roads. If there were no taxes, then there would be no money to run the government or pay for many of the things from which everyone benefits.

Sales Tax

In most states, you pay a tax when you buy something. This tax is called a sales tax. The tax is a portion of the price of the item. If an item costs one dollar and there is a 10 percent sales tax, the real cost is $1.10. This is why if you want to buy something that costs $99.99, you had better have more than $100 (in most cases). There have been taxes on traded goods between countries for centuries.

Though we may not notice it when we make a purchase, the sales tax on everyday items helps to fund state programs.

These taxes were in the form of duties, fees, or tariffs to import goods. Import taxes are paid for by the importer and are usually passed on to the consumer in the price of the item.

In 1929, the stock market crashed, starting a very rough period in American history called the Great Depression. State governments were having a hard time managing their budgets. Many people were out of work. Sales of everything were down. Demand on the states' social systems was incredibly high. In order to offset these costs, many states began adding a sales tax to the purchase of everyday items. By 1970, sales tax was bringing in more money than any other source.[1] After all, people will always buy things. Every time they make a purchase a portion of that purchase goes to the state. The states use the money to pay bills.

Today, there are only five states that do not have a sales tax. Those states are Alaska, Delaware, Montana, New Hampshire, and Oregon.[2] There is no direct sales tax for purchases made on the internet, but many states have found a way to charge businesses. If you sell something on the internet to someone in another state, you may have to pay that state a portion of the sale.

City/State

Many states also charge a tax on income. This tax applies to both people and companies. Some states only tax money made on stocks. Hawaii was the first state to create a state income tax in 1901, even though it was not a state yet![3] Several states had an income tax before there was a federal income tax. During the Great Depression, many states created an income tax to deal with increased pressure on the local government to help people who were hurt by the depression.

The highest state income tax in the United States is in California. California is the only state to charge more than 10 percent. They charge 13.3 percent. This means that most Californians send nearly all the money they earn in January to the state. Of course, this money is spread out over the whole year. Otherwise, Californians would get no money for the month of January! Several states have no income tax. Alaska, Florida, Nevada, South Dakota, Texas, Washington, and Wyoming do not charge income tax, though some of those states do charge taxes on money made from the stock market or business interests.

The largest use for state income taxes is education. In 2016, all the states combined spent $400 billion on teaching kids from kindergarten to high school.[5] Many states provide health care for low income or otherwise dependent residents. The next priority after health care is colleges. The rest of the money is used for providing transportation, helping the poor, and maintaining prisons. There are

Riches from Below

Alaska was one of the early states to start a state income tax. In 1919, Alaska started charging residents a portion of their income. In 1967, the largest oil field in America was discovered in the waters offshore. After a pipeline was built in 1977, billions of dollars rolled into the state accounts. There was so much money Alaska decided to stop charging income tax. Residents of Alaska actually end up getting money from the state just for living there. In 1982, this yearly check was $1,000. It has gone up and down over the years with the price of oil.[4]

State income taxes play a major role in funding education, from kindergarten through high school.

lots of other things on which states spend money, but these are the biggest areas.

National

Since 1913, Americans have had to pay a portion of their income to the federal government. Most income earned in the United States is subject to taxes. Some of the money that citizens earn overseas can also be taxed. If you receive a gift, you may have to pay taxes on the value of the gift. Thankfully, the gift would have to be really big to require taxes. If you receive a big inheritance, you may have to pay taxes on it as well. Finally, there are special taxes that workers

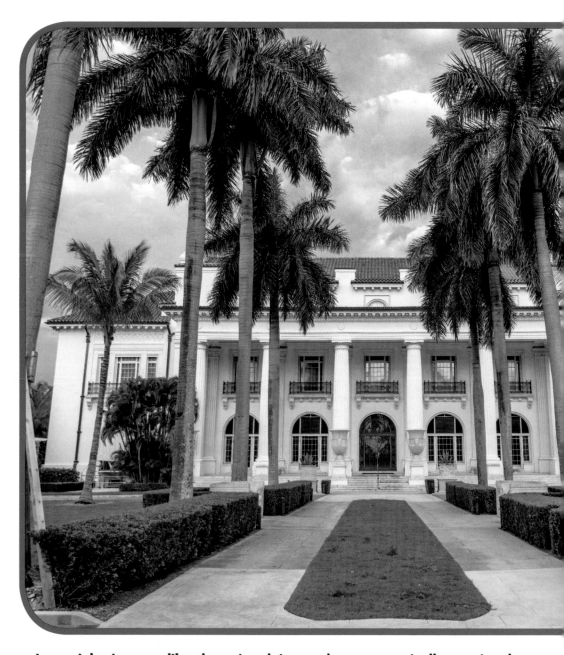

Large inheritances, like those involving real estate, typically require the inheritor to pay taxes.

and their employers must pay. These employment taxes pay for retirement and health insurance for retirees and others who are dependent on the federal government.

People who are very poor usually do not pay taxes. There are a number of programs that even provide money to the poorest people that they can use for anything they want. The idea behind the payments is to try to lessen the effects of poverty. Having children can also reduce your taxes and even let you keep some of your money. Child tax credits vary but are usually around $1,000 per child. Even if you pay no taxes you can sometimes qualify for this money as a credit.

In the next chapter, we'll take a closer look at everything for which taxes pay. The list is long and changes all the time. You might even find tax money being spent on strange things like treadmills for shrimp! This is because the government uses some tax money to fund research on things that may prove beneficial to citizens.

What Are Taxes Used For?

The American government takes in over one trillion dollars each year in taxes. If that sounds like a lot of money, the government has actually spent more than that in recent years. Taxes are used for lots of things that we all use. Some of that money is used to pay for people who cannot work. The government also pays money to seniors for their retirement and health care. Taxes are also used to provide for those who cannot work. The money that the government collects pays the salaries of every person who works for the government, even the president! Congress decides each year how to spend all of the money that comes from taxes. They make a budget that determines how much money goes to each part of the government.

Public Goods

A public good is something that everyone benefits from, whether they contribute to it or not. These public goods are available to all. When one person uses them, it does not keep others from also enjoying them. Even though taxes pay for most public goods, you still benefit even if you pay no taxes. Services like police departments and fire departments protect everyone. They do not charge a fee for their service to the person they help. The same is true of most roads. Unless you are on a toll road, no one makes you pay for every mile of road that you use. There are some new tax plans that think we should pay for roads and other public goods based on usage. They want to work the price of these goods into something like registration.

Considered a public good, the maintenance of most roads and highways is funded by American tax dollars.

Some public goods are less concrete. The government spends money to try to enforce clean air rules and prevent pollution. If you breathe air, you benefit. No one will track your breaths and make you pay back the breath. There are public parks all over the country. Some of the larger ones charge an entry fee, but the playground in your neighborhood costs you nothing. Tax dollars were likely used to buy the land and all the swings and slides. No one checks at the gate to see if you paid your taxes.

Schools are another good example of a public good. From kindergarten through high school, kids do not have to pay to go to a public school. Taxes pay for the school, but some people do not make enough to have to pay taxes. Their children still can go to the school. Public goods like schools are important not only for the individual but also for society. Those who finish school make more money and can pay more taxes to make even better schools.

Health Care and Retirement

After the Civil War, America was facing a big problem. The war had left hundreds of thousands orphaned or widowed.[1] Congress passed a law that paid a stipend to anyone wounded in the war

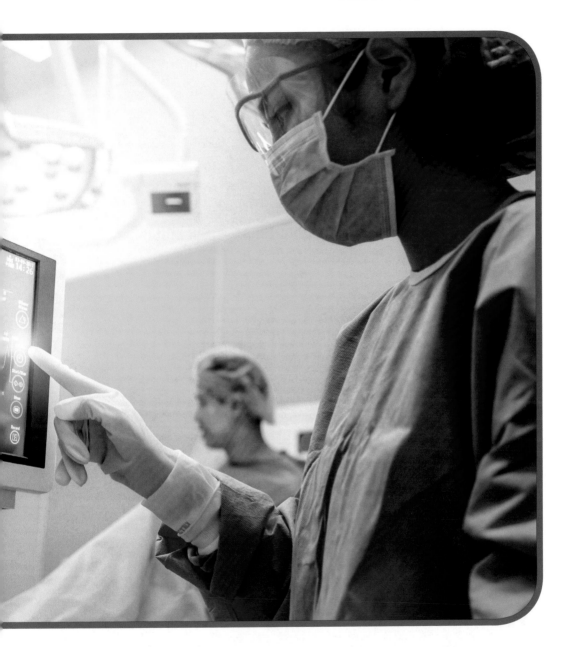

Taxpayer-funded programs like Medicare and Medicaid help lower-income individuals and the elderly afford medical care.

and to any widows or orphans of soldiers who had died in the war. While some companies offered a retirement plan, there was no national retirement plan. In 1935, the United States created a program called Social Security. This program paid retired people money each month. The program also supported those unable to work for physical or mental reasons.

President Franklin Roosevelt originally wanted to include health insurance in his Social Security plan. There were too many people who argued against it. It took until 1965 for a health insurance act to pass.[2] The new health insurance program was known as Medicare.

Health Care for All

Some countries have a national health care system. Citizens pay little or nothing to doctors and hospitals. If they are sick or injured, they receive treatment. Of course, medical care is not free. Systems like this are paid for by higher taxes. Germany has the oldest national health care system. In 1883, Germany passed its Sickness Insurance Law that made sure all citizens could be treated for illness or injury.[3] Some people complain that health care systems like this mean poorer treatment and longer waits. Others say they do not want to pay unless they are sick.

It paid for doctor visits and injury treatment for the elderly. States adopted similar programs known as Medicaid. With the passage of these programs, the poor and elderly were no longer left to fend for themselves.

Social Security and Medicare are paid for through taxes on income. Businesses pay a portion of the tax for each of their employees. The workers pay the rest of the tax each month from their salary. Everyone's taxes are gathered up and used to pay for those who need the benefits. People who work for themselves have to pay the entire tax. For example, a person making $100 would pay

Federal taxes pay for programs like Social Security, which is intended to pay money to people who have retired.

six dollars and their company would pay the other six dollars. A person working for his or herself must pay the whole twelve dollars. Because the number of people paying is more than those in need, there is enough money.

Government

National defense and other government functions cost a lot of money. Everyone benefits from them, so money is taken from taxes to pay for them. The military protects everyone just like police and firemen. Likewise, the government works for everyone. Taxpayers get to choose many government leaders through elections. Run–ning a government and defending the nation are not cheap. In the last three years, Americans spent nearly $2 trillion on the military.[4] That is a two with twelve zeros! The government spends $1.8 trillion each year. That number does not include all of the education and insurance programs we have discussed. That money pays for the day-to-day operations of the government. It pays the salaries and expenses for everyone who works for the United States government.

Our leaders in Washington get paid for their work governing the country. The president gets paid $400,000 each year. The men and women of Congress earn $174,000 each year. Taxes also pay for the salaries of all of the secretaries and other people who work for the government. All of this money comes from taxes that Ameri–cans pay each year. The Department of Treasury receives all of the money from taxes and distributes it to the government based on a budget created by Congress. In the next chapter, we will look at how these taxes get paid.

How Do Taxes Get Paid?

By April 15 of each year, Americans who earn income must pay their taxes. Americans are required to figure out how much tax they owe and pay it to the government every year. The IRS provides the forms and instructions. Many people use the internet to pay their taxes. There are even smartphone applications that let you pay your taxes by phone! Many people get a portion of the taxes they paid during the year back as a refund. Taxes are not optional. If you do not pay your taxes you can be sent to jail.

Filing Taxes

Each year, Americans who earn income must file a tax return with the IRS by April 15. The IRS provides a variety of different forms depending on how complicated your taxes are. Usually, you can pick up the forms for free at any post office. If you make more than $10,000, you may have to file an income tax return. The amount varies with age and can depend on whether or not you are married. Married people can combine their money, so their minimum amount

Unless they request an extension, all Americans must file their tax forms by April 15 each year.

is around $20,000. Widows and widowers are allowed to earn a little more than single people do before having to file a return.

In most cases, the money that you earn has already been reported to the IRS. If you work for a company, you receive a form called a W-2 that tells you how much you earned and how much you have already paid in taxes. If the money came from a source that did not take any taxes you will receive a form called a 1099. These forms let you know how much income was reported to the government. When you file your taxes, if you claim a different amount, the IRS may take a closer look. If the IRS wants to double-check your taxes, they perform an audit. An audit is like an interview in which you must prove that your information is correct.

Many people complete the forms by themselves and submit them to the IRS. Most companies use an accountant to file their taxes. Some people have very complicated tax returns, so they also use an accountant. Even though an accountant might prepare and submit your taxes, it is still your responsibility if something is wrong. If you need more time to submit your taxes, you can request to send your return in late. If you owe money, then you also will have to pay interest if you delay payment beyond April 15.

Refunds

Companies take a portion of every employee's paycheck and send it to the government as taxes. These taxes are estimated based on what the employee is expected to earn during the year. The amount taken also depends on how many people depend on the worker. Family members count as deductions. Each year, employees calculate how much they owe the United States government.

Occasionally, individuals pay more in taxes than they should have. When this happens, the state or federal government sends them a refund check.

They use the tax forms to compare the amount they owe with the amount they have already paid. If they paid less than they should have, they must make a payment of the remaining amount by April 15. If a person paid more than they should have, then they get the extra money back in a refund. They can only get a refund if they have no leftover tax debt from the previous year. It is also possible for the courts or government to take any refund if the person owes money because of a crime or settlement.

It is possible to get a refund even for people who do not pay any taxes. This is because there are many deductions for low income families. One of the most common deductions is a child tax credit. If a family has a child under the age of seventeen, they are allowed to deduct $1,000 from the amount they owe the government in taxes. If the family owes less than $1,000, they can get the difference back as a refund. Families with multiple children can end up with a few thousand dollars as a refund through this credit and others aimed specifically at low-income families. The earned income credit is a refund that gives the lowest earners extra money to try to

Is it Deductible?

There are many things a person buys or spends money on that can be deducted. When a valid expense is deducted, the money spent on the item is not taxable. Deductions are for necessary expenses for businesses and people. Some people get very creative about what they want to deduct. Many things required by doctors can be deducted, even a swimming pool or a program to quit smoking. Just don't try to claim hair plugs or Botox! The expense must be reasonable and necessary. One man tried to claim a trip to Brazil because he bought spatulas there for his restaurant.[1]

combat poverty in America. Each year, millions of Americans get a refund check.

Tax Evasion

Paying taxes is not optional. Anyone who fails to pay taxes or tries to claim expenses that are not justified can wind up in a courtroom or a jail cell. One of the most famous tax evasion cases in history is Al Capone's. Al Capone was a gangster that was responsible for all kinds of crimes, including murder. The problem was that no one could find any proof he was committing these crimes. Finally, the government figured out how to get the gangster. He was spending way more money than the income he was claiming could possibly support. Al Capone was convicted of tax evasion and failing to file a tax return and was sentenced to eleven years in prison.[2] The IRS was able to get the worst criminal in America off the street just because he wasn't following their rules!

While calculating, filing, and mailing your taxes can be stressful, it's an essential part of being an American citizen.

What Does a Taxpayer Do?

Taxes can be difficult. After all, there are people who spend their whole careers just working on taxes and tax issues. Taxes are an important part of a functioning government. Taxpayers are the most important part of that system. Without their contributions each year, the government could not run. We would also not enjoy many of the public benefits like roads, schools, and a military to keep us safe. The next time you see a tax on your receipt or a paycheck, you can rest assured that you are helping lots of people with your contribution.

CHAPTER NOTES

Chapter 1: History of Taxes

1. Ron Chernow, *Alexander Hamilton*, New York, NY: Penguin Books, 2005.
2. Andrew Beattie, "A Short History of Taxes," Forbes.com, April 14, 2010, https://www.forbes.com/2010/04/14/tax-history-law-personal-finance-tax-law-changes.html.
3. "The Agency, its Mission and Statutory Authority," IRS.gov. https://www.irs.gov/about-irs/the-agency-its-mission-and-statutory-authority.

Chapter 2: Who Pays Taxes?

1. Albert Henry Smyth. *The Writings of Benjamin Franklin, Vol. X (1789–1790)* (New York, NY: MacMillan, 1970), p. 69.
2. "The Minimum Freelancers Need to Earn to File Income Taxes," FreelanceTaxation.com, https://www.freelancetaxation.com/the-minimum-freelancers-need-to-earn-in-order-to-have-to-file-income-taxes.
3. Alina Tugend, "Donations to Religious Institutions Fall as Values Change," *New York Times*, November 3, 2016, https://www.nytimes.com/2016/11/06/giving/donations-to-religious-institutions-fall-as-values-change.html.

Chapter 3: Types of Taxes

1. Mark Faggiano, "The History of Sales Tax in the United States," Tax Jar, July 23, 2014, https://blog.taxjar.com/history-sales-tax-united-states/.
2. Ibid.
3. Scott Drenkard, "When Did Your State Adopt Its Income Tax?" Tax Foundation, June 10, 2014, https://taxfoundation.org/when-did-your-state-adopt-its-income-tax/.

4. Rory Carroll, "Alaska residents to receive record payment from oil royalty fund," Reuters, September 16, 2015, https://www.reuters.com/article/alaska-payment-fund/alaska-residents-to-receive-record-payment-from-oil-royalty-fund-idUSL1N11N03U20150917.

5. "Policy Basics: Where Do Our State Tax Dollars Go?" Center on Budget and Policy Priorities, April 24, 2017. https://www.cbpp.org/research/state-budget-and-tax/policy-basics-where-do-our-state-tax-dollars-go.

Chapter 4: What Are Taxes Used For?

1. "Historical Background and Development of Social Security," Social Security Administration, https://www.ssa.gov/history/briefhistory3.html.

2. Julian E. Zelizer, "How Medicare Was Made," *New Yorker*, February 15, 2015, https://www.newyorker.com/news/news-desk/medicare-made.

3. Abe Bortz, "Social Security: A Brief History of Social Insurance," Virginia Commonwealth University, https://socialwelfare.library.vcu.edu/social-security/social-security-a-brief-history-of-social-insurance/.

4. Office of the Undersecretary of Defense (Comptroller), "National Defense Budget Estimates, 2018," Department of Defense, August 2017, http://comptroller.defense.gov/Portals/45/Documents/defbudget/fy2018/FY18_Green_Book.pdf.

Chapter 5: How Do Taxes Get Paid?

1. "The Comprehensive List of Odd Tax Deductions," Kars4Kids.com, December 20, 2013, https://www.kars4kids.org/blog/the-comprehensive-list-of-odd-tax-deductions/.

2. Angela Bryson, "History's Most Famous IRS Cases," Bryson Law Group, 2017, https://www.brysonlawfirm.com/news/item/290-historys-most-famous-irs-cases.html.

GLOSSARY

accountant A person whose job it is to manage others' money and help them file taxes.

barter To trade one good or service for another.

deduction Something you've spent money on that helps lower the amount of taxes you pay at the end of the year. Business expenses, like office supplies, or health care costs, like prescription medications, can be used as deductions.

IRS Internal Revenue Service; the government agency responsible for the taxation of American citizens.

Medicaid A health care system run by the states that helps low-income citizens get the health care they need.

Medicare A health care system run by the federal government that helps elderly citizens get the health care they need.

nonprofit A business that does charitable work and is therefore taxed differently than a traditional business.

public good Something that is paid for with taxpayer money and that benefits the broader community, such as schools and roads.

stipend A form of income that is paid to help someone cover his or her living expenses.

tariff A tax on goods that are imported or exported.

taxes Money that citizens pay to the government to help pay for public goods like schools and roads.

What Does a Taxpayer Do?

taxpayer A person who pays taxes.

tax return A document sent to the IRS declaring a citizen's income and paying his or her taxes for the year.

1099 A form from the IRS that citizens use to report their income to the government.

W-2 A form used by businesses to report their employees' wages, and the taxes withheld from them, to the government.

FURTHER READING

Books

Andal, Walter. *Finance 101 for Kids: Money Lessons Children Cannot Afford to Miss*. Minneapolis, MN: Mill City Press, 2016.

McGillen, Jamie Kyle. *The Kids' Money Book: Earning, Saving, Spending, Investing, Donating*. New York, NY: Sterling Childrens Books, 2016.

Minden, Cecilia. *Understanding Taxes*. Ann Arbor, MI: Cherry Lake Publishing, 2014.

Tyson, Eric. *Personal Finance for Dummies*. Hoboken, NJ: John Wiley & Sons, 2016.

Websites

Internal Revenue Service
www.irs.gov
The government agency responsible for managing the American tax system.

Investopedia
www.investopedia.com
A website that explains taxes and finance with information that everyone from individual taxpayers to corporate accountants can use.

INDEX